Resistance is not futile.

CONTENTS

KAMUI [6] Shingo Nanami

KAMUI
カムイ
6
七海慎吾
Shingo Nanami

KAMUI

BY SHINGO NANAMI

6

brought to you by
BROCCOLI BOOKS
A DIVISION OF BROCCOLI INTERNATIONAL USA

KAMUI Volume 6

English Adaptation Staff
Translation: Satsuki Yamashita
English Adaptation: Elizabeth Hanel
Touch-Up & Lettering: Keiran O'Leary
Cover & Graphic Supervision: Christopher McDougall
Graphic Assistant: Krystal Sae Eua

Editor: Dietrich Seto
Sales Manager: Ardith D. Santiago
Managing Editor: Shizuki Yamashita
Publisher: Kaname Tezuka

Email: editor@broccolibooks.com
Website: www.bro-usa.com

A BROCCOLI BOOKS Manga
Broccoli Books is a division of Broccoli International USA, Inc.
1728 S. La Cienega Blvd., Los Angeles, CA 90035

ISBN-13: 978-1-5974-1053-3
ISBN-10: 1-5974-1053-5

Published by Broccoli International USA, Inc.
First printing, December 2006

All illustrations by Shingo Nanami.

Distributed by Publishers Group West

ANIME GAMERS
BROCCOLI INTERNATIONAL USA
www.bro-usa.com

10 9 8 7 6 5 4 3 2 1
Printed in Canada

KAMUI

TABLE OF CONTENTS

6

CHARACTERS

カムイ

ATSUMA
A young man who is sent by his village in the north to retrieve the stolen sacred spirit, Okikurumi. He is infused with the spirit of an ancient sword.

KOJOMARU
The Kamui of an ancient sword from Atsuma's village. In return for the use of his powers, Atsuma allows Kojomaru to fuse with his body. Despite his ability and age, he is both short-tempered and immature.

UTSUHO
The man who betrayed Atsuma and took Okikurumi from his village.

SUMIRE
NOA's second-in-command and Tensho (Commander of the Heaven Division). She is infused with the power of the wind.

SHUI
Second lieutenant of NOA who takes Atsuma under his wing. He is infused with the power of fire.

CHARACTERS カムイ

SHIKI
The top general of NOA. Despite assuming an air of royalty, he is unemotional.

AIKA
First lieutenant of NOA and Sumire's right-hand woman. She appears to be strict and uncaring, which comes from her reluctance to trust anyone but Sumire.

HYDE
Lieutenant general of NOA, he holds the number three position behind Sumire. As the Chisho, he is in charge of the Earth Division.

YANAGI
First lieutenant of NOA and Hyde's right-hand man. Although loyal to Hyde, he keeps in close contact with Shiki.

ANZU
Teenage cadet at NOA. She joins after her family dies in the earthquakes, but is actually scared of fighting and only wants to live a normal life.

TERMINOLOGY

カムイ

Atanan - Monsters that suddenly appeared after the Grand Sinker.

Earth and Sky Division - The Earth Division is led by Chisho (Commander) Hyde, and the Sky Division is led by Tensho (Commander) Sumire. The Sky Division and the Earth Division are the two forces that form NOA's military strength. Although their names are Earth and Sky, this has no relation to their jurisdiction.

EDEN - A part of the former city of Tokyo that was protected from the earthquakes by the government research facility's barrier. It is now controlled by NOA.

Ekashi – A term meaning "elders."

Grand Sinker - The second of two great earthquakes that have left Japan devastated. The southernmost islands of Kyushu and Shikoku are both completely submerged, and a good percentage of the main island Honshu is left underwater.

KAMUI - A term used to refer to the spirits.

I'touren - A term referring to the spirit embodied by members of NOA. For example, Lady Sumire embodies the wind i'touren.

NOA - Stands for Noble Offensive Academy. It is a society of young men and women who have been infused with kamui in order to fight the atanan. It is backed by a government research facility that has been performing paranormal experiments on humans.

Okikurumi - An ancient spirit and the most sacred kamui that is stolen from Atsuma's village. Its disappearance has a key role in the recent natural disasters and appearance of the atanan.

Tohsu - A term used to refer to the powers used by members of NOA.

Chapter
25 reason to resist

KAMUI 6

Shingo Nanami

THROB
STUBBORN...
...AS USUAL.
ATSUMA-KUN.
Huff

HMPH
BUT...
SHINE
IT WILL JUST HURT YOU MORE...
...IF YOU KEEP EXERTING THAT WOUNDED BODY.
YOU'RE THE ONE WHO SAID YOU COULDN'T DO ANYTHING.
drip
drop
SO WHY DO YOU...
...RESIST NOW?
IT'S TRUE...
...THAT I'M FREE OF KOJOMARU.
BUT THIS ISN'T...
...THE FREEDOM I LONGED FOR.

WHY DO I RESIST?
MAYBE I CAN'T STAND UP TO YOU OR SAVE THE WORLD.
BUT IF I DO NOTHING,
I CAN NEVER FORGIVE MYSELF.
I MIGHT AS WELL LET YOU KILL ME.
GRIP
I CAN'T...
WHO TAUGHT ME...
...LIE TO MYSELF...
...ANYMORE.

SO YOU...
...DON'T PLAN ON GIVING UP QUIETLY, THEN.
REACH
I DON'T MIND...
...TAKING MY TIME WITH YOU.
LIFT
WELL,
THAT IS A PROBLEM, ISN'T IT LORD HYDE?

THAT GUY.
HE WAS...
...AT THE PARTY...
OH,
IT'S SO NICE THAT YOU REMEMBERED HIM.
WOOOOO
AFTER HE LOST TO YOU AT THE HALL,
HE WAS GOING TO BE DISPOSED OF.
THUD
SO I DECIDED TO TAKE HIM IN AND RE-USE HIM.
URGH!
Grab

AGH!
GRAB
HE'S TOO STRONG!
COUGH
WHY...
...DID YOU...
WHY?
BECAUSE HE AND ALL NOA ARE RESEARCH FACILITY PROPERTY.
WASTE NOT, WANT NOT.
CLENCH
BESIDES,
HE'S A SPECIAL GIFT FROM UTSUHO...
CLENCH
... TO KEEP ME SAFE IN NOA SINCE I DON'T HAVE TOHSU.

SINCE I TOOK SPECIAL CARE OF HIM AT NOA,
TAP
SO I CAN'T THROW HIM AWAY JUST YET.
HE NEEDS TO PAY ME BACK WITH HIS LIFE.
I THINK HE'S BECOME STRONGER...
...NOW THAT HE DOESN'T HAVE A BRAIN TO WORRY WITH.
SO? DO YOU WANT TO CHANGE YOUR MIND?
SQUEEZE
WHO...
...SAID...
...I'D CHANGE MY MIND?

AGH!
AH!
AHH!
I DON'T MIND.
WE HAVE PLENTY OF TIME.

Wheeze
Haha
JUST FOR THAT LOVELY PERFORMANCE,
I'LL TELL YOU A SECRET.
TAP
KICK
KICK
TAP
NOA MAY HAVE CRUMBLED TO NOTHING,
WITH THE GROWTH OF OKIKURUMI.
BUT THAT JUST MEANS THAT THE ACADEMY DISAPPEARED.
CLICK
THE STUDENTS OF NOA...
... ARE NOT DEAD.

THEY'RE...
BA-
DUM
...NOT DEAD?
LIFT
LORD HYDE IS A PERFECT EXAMPLE.
THOSE SWALLOWED BY OKIKU-RUMI...
...LOSE THEIR TOHSU AND THEIR SELF.
WHAM
BUT THEY DON'T DIE.
WHAM

SLAM
THUD
SO YOUR FRIENDS...
SWIPE
...WILL PROBABLY...
...LAST LONGER THAN YOU.
Haa haa
Ha ha
BUT REMEMBER.
EVEN IF THEY DON'T KNOW WHO THEY ARE...
...AND DON'T HAVE THE POWER TO LIFT A FINGER,
THEY WILL CONTINUE TO LIVE AS PART OF OKIKURUMI FOR ALL ETERNITY.

I GOTTA GO...
...FOR A WHILE.
WHO SAID THAT...
...TO ME?
twitch

STAND
THEY CAN'T FEEL PAIN ANYMORE.
SO WE SHOULD HURRY TO END YOUR SUFFERING, TOO.
Whoosh
WHAM
CATCH
HAVE YOU BEEN...
...LISTENING TO ME?
STRAIGHTEN

YEAH.
COUGH
AND I REMEMBERED SOMETHING ELSE.
I WON'T LEAVE YOU BEHIND.
I DIDN'T ...
... BELIEVE THOSE WORDS BEFORE.
SO DON'T WORRY!
BUT IF HE'S NOT DEAD,
MAYBE I SHOULD RE-CONSIDER THEM AGAIN.
......
......
I THOUGHT I LOST EVERY-THING.
Wheeze

I WASN'T PLANNING TO DO ANY-THING.
I DIDN'T EVEN...
...LET MYSELF THINK.
I THOUGHT THIS WAS THE END.
THE FINAL CHAIN ON MY HEART.
BUT THAT ISN'T THE TRUTH.
BUT THE WORDS AND MEMORIES INSIDE OF ME,
ARE TRYING TO MAKE THIS BODY MOVE.

YOUR WORDS MEAN NOTHING TO ME.
WHY DO I RESIST?
I DON'T WANT THE ILLUSION OF FREEDOM.
Wheeze
IF I CAN'T EVEN SEE...
...WHAT'S RIGHT IN FRONT OF ME,
THEN I CAN'T BE MY TRUE SELF!
TO REMEMBER MYSELF!

I STILL DON'T KNOW...
...HOW TO UNLOCK THE CHAINS ON MY HEART.
I WANT TRUE FREEDOM.
EVEN IF I DON'T HAVE TOHSU, AND I DON'T KNOW HOW TO GO ON,
EVEN IF I SUFFER, EVEN IF I GET WOUNDED FURTHER,
I DON'T WANT TO STAND STILL.

IF I AT LEAST KEEP MOVING...
WHOOSH
THUD
...MY VISION WILL BECOME CLEAR.
ALMOST UNTIL...
...I CAN FORGET THE PAIN.
HUFF

THIS BODY...
...IS ALL I HAVE.
HUFF
MOVE.
NO MATTER HOW WEAK.
I WILL GO AS FAR AS I CAN.
JUST TO PROVE I'M ALIVE!

MOVE...
GLINT
MOVE!
RING

RING
Huff
IS THIS...
...SYNCHRONIZATION?
IS THIS WAVE ATSUMA?
Huff
I'VE NEVER FELT...
...ANYTHING LIKE THIS BEFORE.
SHUDDER

Pierce
OW!
WHERE DID THIS WOUND COME FROM?
WHAT ARE YOU DOING, ATSUMA?
TUG
AND WHAT IS THIS?
IT'S NUMB FROM THE DRUG, BUT...
...WHAT'S CAUSING IT?
Clench
TSK

TAP
THIS LADY'S CONSCIOUSNESS IS WEAK, SO SHE WON'T BOTHER ME ANYMORE.
BUT I HAVE TO HURRY AND FIND THE SWORD.
THIS IS A WEIRD FEELING. I FEEL LIKE I'M GOING TO LOSE CONSCIOUSNESS.
TAP
GEEZ.
THIS LADY AND ATSUMA...
...ARE...
...TOTAL PAINS.
...MIRE...

A VOICE.
...DY...
...SUMI...
THIS IS...
...OKIKURUMI'S WAVE.
TAP
...ADY...
...SUMIR...
IT'S CALLING FOR THIS LADY?
TAP

BEHIND THIS GATE?
Whirr
Thump
URGH
Wince
WHOM

!
ROAR
HUFF
CRUMBLE
CRUMBLE

WHAT'S THIS?
ROAR

THE BASE OF OKIKURUMI.
BA-DUM
RING
OH!
BA-DUM
FLOAT
THE SWORD!
RING

WHEN EVERYTHING FELL APART, IT MUST HAVE GOTTEN TANGLED UP HERE.
I CAN GO BACK NOW.
GLOP
BUT WHAT...
...WAS THAT VOICE?

WHAT?
SHOOT!
THIS LADY...
URGH!
SHE'S FOOD FOR OKIKURUMI.
GRIP
...MIRE.
LADY SUMIRE.
THIS VOICE.
THE WAVE...
...IS VERY SIMILAR TO OKIKURUMI.

IT CAN'T BE.
...MIRE.
WHO IS CALLING THIS LADY?
LET GO!
CRACK
AGH!
...DY SUMIRE.
GLOP
GLOP
I CAN'T...
...BE CAUGHT HERE LIKE THIS!
GLOP
I HAVE TO...
...HURRY UP AND GET BACK.
IF I'M...

...NOT...
...THERE...
CRUMBLE
LADY...
SUMIRE...
TRING
PLEASE...

...SAVE...
...LADY...
WHIRR
...SUMIRE!
SLASH
ROAR

ROAR
TOHSU...
CLINK
...OF FIRE?
ROAR

SOMEONE WAS CALLING ME.
A WAVE THAT'S LIKE LIGHT.
WHO WISHES...
...TO RETURN?

ROAR
ROAR
BOOM
!!
BOOM
THIS WAVE!
IT CAN'T BE!
RIP
WHOSE SIDE...
RIP

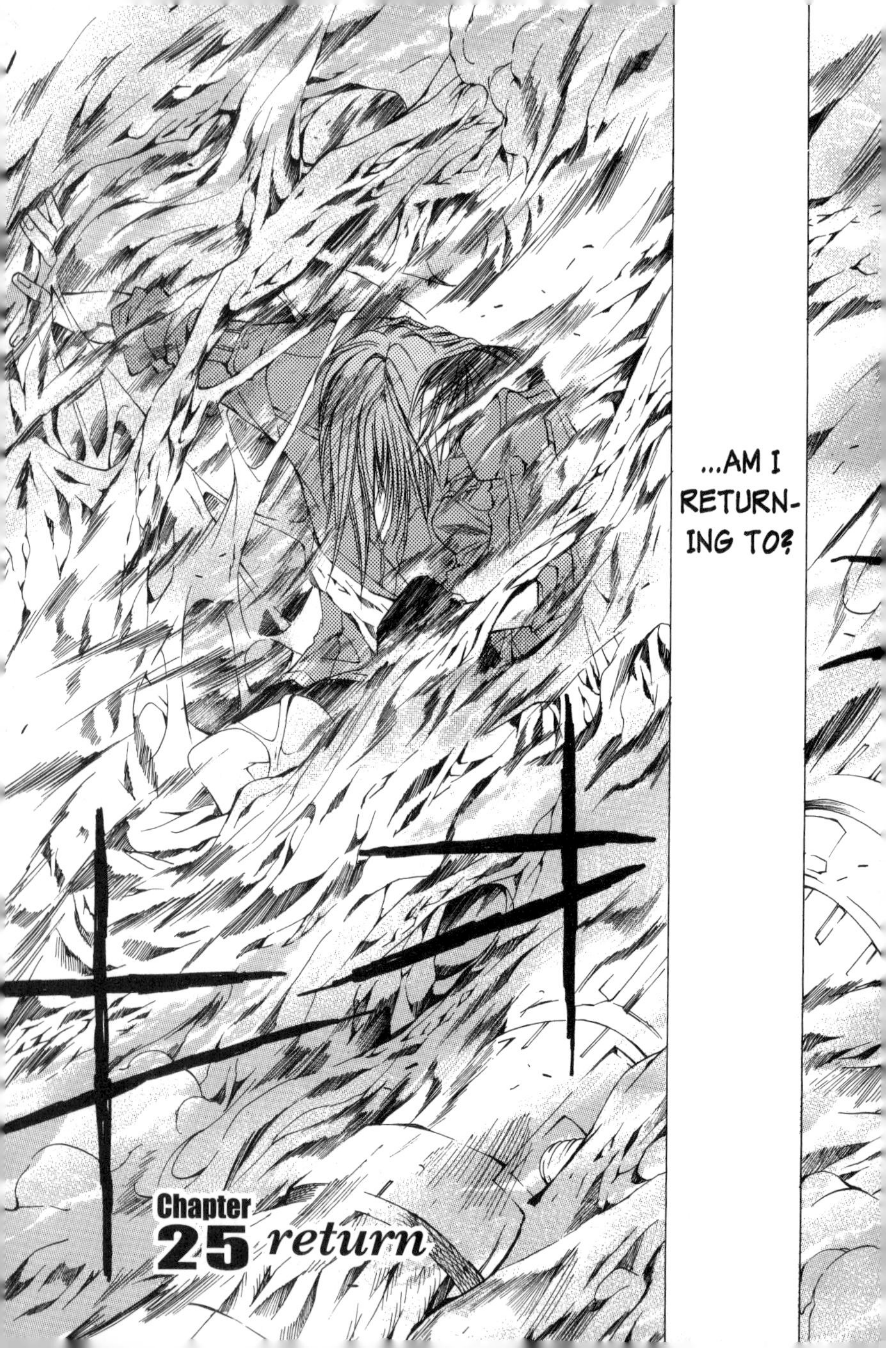
...AM I RETURNING TO?
Chapter 25 return

—!......
HOW?

WHY ARE YOU ALIVE?
ROAR
YOU WERE SWALLOWED BY OKIKU-RUMI.
YOU BECAME ITS FOOD.
HOW CAN YOU HAVE ANY POWER LEFT?
roar
GRIN
I DUNNO.

THUD
HUH!
WHOA...
Splash
WOBBLE
OH, OW.
MY BODY IS SO SORE.

ACTUALLY, I HAVE SOME QUESTIONS TOO.
I DON'T REMEMBER ANYTHING AFTER I JUMPED IN AFTER HER.
I JUST WOKE UP NOW.
I SAVED YOU THINKING YOU WERE LADY SUMIRE.
BUT YOU'RE SOMEONE ELSE.
roar
THIS DOESN'T LOOK LIKE NOA ANYMORE.
AND THIS OKIKURUMI TURNED INTO SOMETHING FREAKY.
WELL, I CAN FIND OUT...
...THOSE THINGS LATER.
Flutter

WHAT HAPPENED TO ATSUMA?
STIFFEN

CLENCH
I DON'T KNOW.
roar
I DON'T KNOW.
WHY DO YOU SHOW UP NOW?
THERE'S NO NEED FOR YOU TO KNOW ANYTHING ELSE.
YOU ALREADY FOUND...
...WHAT YOU WERE LOOKING FOR!
—...

CUZ...
STRAIGHTFORWARD
...I WOKE UP.
ALL BECAUSE OF...
...YOU!
......!?
I CAME TO THE DEEPEST PARTS OF NOA LOOKING FOR THE TRUTH.
roar
I DON'T KNOW HOW LONG IT'S BEEN...
... OR HOW YOU ENDED UP INSIDE LADY SUMIRE.
BUT WHEN YOU BROUGHT HER HERE,
SOMETHING INSIDE AIKA STARTED STIRRING.
SETTLE

EVEN UNCONSCIOUS, I FELT IT.
PLEASE...
I HEARD A VOICE.
...SAVE...
...LADY SUMIRE...
THE NAME SHE WAS CALLING...
...WASN'T MINE.
BUT I WOKE UP ANYWAY.
BESIDES...
STAND

...WHEN I SAY I'LL BE BACK...
...I COME BACK.
TO HIS SIDE.

I FIGURED YOU'RE THINKING IT'S NONE OF MY BUSINESS. BUT THAT'S FUN TOO.
YOU'RE IN THE WAY.
THAT VOICE...
...IS A NUISANCE.
BOTH TO ME AND ATSUMA!
WHY DON'T YOU JUST WAIT HERE WITH THAT LADY?
THE GENERAL GUY IS HERE TOO.
ONCE I TAKE BACK OKIKURUMI,
I'LL KILL ALL OF YOU!

CLANG
!?
THERE SHE IS!
REPORT TO LORD SHIKI!
HOLD HER HERE UNTIL THEN!
click
click
glint
click
TSK
BAM
BAM
BAM
Vrrrrm
WHOA!

HEY!
WAIT A SEC, KOJO...
FLOAT
SLASH
AH...
AGHHH!
ROAR

THUD
THUD
THUD
WHAT'S GOING ON?
Sizzle
I AM SO CONFUSED, MY LADY.
ALL I KNOW NOW...
Well, I kinda knew it
From the party.
...IS THAT THE KAMUI DOESN'T LIKE ME.
ROLL
AND THAT THE SOLDIERS OF THE RESEARCH FACILITY,
WORE UNIFORMS SIMILAR TO THIS.

splash
splash
So...
WHAT SHOULD WE DO, BOSS LADY?
WE CAN'T TAKE A NAP,
NOW THAT WE'RE FREE.
I DON'T FEEL ATSUMA'S WAVE NEARBY, EITHER.
BUT I'LL STAY HERE UNTIL YOU WAKE UP.
IF I CARRIED YOU AROUND WITHOUT YOUR PERMISSION,
YOU'D BE REALLY MAD.

HOW LONG HAS IT BEEN SINCE I'VE WATCHED YOU SLEEP?
I GUESS WE CAN'T GO BACK TO THOSE DAYS...
...WITHOUT GETTING HURT ALL OVER AGAIN.
THERE'S A LIGHT...
...CALLING...
HEY, CAN YOU...
...HEAR MY VOICE?
...FROM FAR AWAY.

WHEN...
...I FOUND YOU IN THAT WET MESS,
EVEN AS I WAS LOSING CONSCIOUS-NESS,
I THOUGHT IT MIGHT BE A DREAM...
...BUT...
YOU WEREN'T MOVING.

...YOU SAVED ME...
...FROM BEING COMPLETELY DEVOURED.
SO IT LOOKS LIKE I'M THE ONLY ONE WHO WAS SAVED.
roar
I DON'T KNOW WHY YOU DID THAT.
IF YOU TELL ME TO PROTECT LADY SUMIRE WITH THIS POWER, I WILL.
BUT IT WON'T MEAN ANYTHING TO ME.

WHO?
YOU'RE THE ONE WHO TOLD ME I'M STUBBORN.
I CAN'T DO ANYTHING ELSE.
BUT IT'S WRONG FOR YOU TO JUST GIVE UP NOW.
THAT WOULD BE A WASTE.
TOUCH
EVEN IF YOU SENT ME AWAY, I WOULDN'T FORGET YOU.
EVEN IF IT MEANS BATTLING OKIKURUMI ITSELF, I SWEAR IT.
A WARM...
...LIGHT.
WHO IS THAT?

WHO...
...ARE YOU?
I LIVE FOR YOU.
PLEASE OPEN YOUR EYES AND GET UP.
I'M HERE...
WHO AM I?
...FOR YOU.

AIKA.

!
Y...
YOU'RE...
WOAH.
WHAT'S WITH YOU?
YOU ALWAYS DID WAKE UP FAST.
BUT THIS TIME...
...YOU'RE TOO LATE.

GRAB

WANT TO GO BACK?
TO WHERE?
I HAVE A LOT...
...TO ASK YOU...
...TO SAY TO YOU.

THERE ARE TOO MANY THINGS.
SO JUST TELL ME ONE THING.
THE VOICE THAT'S CALLING ME.
THE WARM LIGHT.
WHERE DO YOU WANT TO GO?

WHOSE SIDE...
...DO I WANT TO RETURN TO?
SU...
...MI...
...RE?

OKAY.
THROB
WHOSE...

...SIDE?
I HEARD THAT THE INTRUDER...
...ESCAPED UNHARMED.
I WOULD LIKE TO THANK YOU,
FOR A JOB WELL DONE.
BUT WHY DO YOU LOOK SO UPSET?
YOU'RE NOT GOING TO TELL ME...
...THAT YOU'RE WORRIED ABOUT THE INTRUDER NOW?

WHAT ARE YOU SAYING?
YOU CHOSE TO RETURN TO THE RESEARCH FACILITY.
SO ALL I ASK IS THAT YOU WORK TO PLEASE ME.
IF YOU CAN'T GET RID OF ONE INTRUDER, THAT'S A PROBLEM.
UNLESS YOU HAVE SOME OTHER REASON...
...FOR INSTANCE...
IF YOU'RE HELPING THE RESEARCH FACILITY TO MAKE MY WISH COME TRUE...
...AND IF THAT'S THE SUREST WAY FOR YOU TO GET WHAT YOU WANT.
EVEN IF THAT IS YOUR MOTIVATION ...

AUGH
...I STILL CONSIDER...
...YOU LOYAL TO ME.
YOU ARE...
BEEP
Urgent call for Lord Shiki.
We have escapees from Tower A Line 01 of the lowest section of the tower.
We are currently pursuing them with the auto guard system and mobile troops.
We will send the data as soon as we confirm their identities.

NOTHING WILL ESCAPE MY GRASP.
NOT YOU, NOT THE WORLD, NOT ANYTHING.
BEEP
SHUI TACHIBANA
AGE/18 SEX/MALE
BLOODTYPE/O
ABILITY/AFFILIATION OF THE FLAME
CAPACITY/RANK-S---SUPERIOR
EXPERIENCE/SEE P.02
Experiment number 0024757. Progress is very superior from the initial stage of an experiment. There are not a personality disorder, a body functional stop, a memory disorder, etc., they show very high capability, and are excellent also in results after dispatch as a member.
I WANT TO ENJOY THIS, SHIKI.
FOR AS LONG AS I CAN.

LADY SUMIRE.
WHENEVER I CALLED HER NAME, I FELT SECURE.
I WAS JUST HAPPY,
TO BE BY HER SIDE.
BUT,
FOR SOME REASON...
...I WAS ALSO AFRAID.

Chapter 27 light

KAMUI 6

Shingo
Nanami

BEEP
BEEP
ROAR
ARGH!
OH, DAMMIT!

ROAR
YOU GUYS ARE GETTING ON MY NERVES!
Huff
!!

!!
PANG
PANG
WHENEVER I USE TOHSU, MY BODY HURTS.
OR IS THIS THE RESULT OF BEING INSIDE OKIKURUMI?
WAS SOME OF MY ENERGY SUCKED OUT OF ME?
Oww...
AM I JUST SORE?
tap
ARGH!
THUD
WHAT IS THIS?
UGH!
......
YEAH,
THAT'S RIGHT.

THIS IS NOTHING...
...COMPARED TO WHAT HAPPENED TO YOU,
OR THE OTHER STUDENTS.
WE CAN'T...
...LEAVE THEM LIKE THAT.
I DON'T...
...WANT TO SEE...
GRIP

...HIS FACE FULL OF PAIN...
...LIKE THAT TIME AT THE PARTY.
WE LOST...
...EVERYTHING.
THERE WAS NO GUARANTEE...
...THAT THOSE DAYS AT NOA WOULD LAST FOREVER.
ESPECIALLY IF...
...THIS WAS PLANNED BY THE RESEARCH FACILITY ALL ALONG.
YOU AND OTHERS HAVE COMPLETELY CHANGED.

BUT WE...
...WEREN'T LIVING JUST TO HAVE EVERYTHING DESTROYED.
THERE WERE SOME THINGS THAT WE GAINED,
AND SOME THINGS THAT DIDN'T CHANGE.
IF HE...
...HAS NOTHING...
...I HAVE TO...
...GO BACK AND BE WITH HIM NO MATTER WHAT.
SOME-THING TO REACH FOR.
SOMETHING RELIABLE.
PLUS...

TWITCH
...YOU WANT TO GO BACK TOO, RIGHT?
Huh?
TO LADY SUMIRE?
THROB
GRIN
Ow, I'm still hurting.
HE SAID...
tap
tap
...SOMETHING TO ME.

THAT YOU WOULD NEVER CHANGE BACK TO YOUR OLD SELF.
THE REASON WHY YOU ARE LOYAL TO LADY SUMIRE,
IS BECAUSE THE IMPRINTING NATURE OF OKIKURUMI AFFECTED YOU.
I DIDN'T...
...KNOW THAT.
tap
BUT NOW THAT I DO,
WHAT CAN I DO ANYWAY?
I DON'T KNOW WHY YOU WERE THE ONLY ONE AFFECTED.
tap
TAP
BUT...
...AT THE SAME TIME...

...I WAS RELIEVED.
BECAUSE...
...YOU WERE HAPPY...
...BEING BY LADY SUMIRE'S SIDE, RIGHT?
HAPPY?

BEING BY HER SIDE...
BA-DUM
...MADE ME HAPPY.
WELL.
BA-DUM
I CAN'T AGREE WITH WHAT THE RESEARCH FACILITY DID.
AND I CAN'T FORGET WHO YOU WERE BEFORE.
I DON'T KNOW WHY YOU ENDED UP JOINING NOA.
BUT IF YOU MADE THE CHOICE TO BE HERE,
AND IF YOU WERE HAPPY HERE,
AND YOU HAVE THE WILL TO LIVE,
AND HAVEN'T FORGOTTEN HER NAME...
IF I HAD KNOWN ALL THIS...

BUT I WAS...
...THEN I WOULD HAVE TOLD YOU...
...THAT THE PAST DOESN'T MATTER.
BA-DUM
...ALWAYS SCARED.
BECAUSE...
...THOSE GENTLE, SAD EYES THAT LOOKED AT ME...
BA-DUM

...I KNEW THAT...
...THEY WERE ALWAYS THERE.
AIKA?

TAP
Shiver
ARE YOU TIRED?
はっ
SLAP
WHAT'S WRONG?
BECAUSE IT WAS TOO MUCH, I LEFT.
TAP
タッ
AIKA!
I WAS SCARED...

...TO BE NEAR HIM.
CLICK
ROAR
THERE THEY ARE!
!
TSK
bang
bang
URGH
ARGH!
IF I STAYED NEAR HIM...
...I WOULD HURT HIM!

WHERE SHOULD I GO?
IF I GO BACK TO HER...
...IT WOULD JUST BE THE SAME...
...BUT WHERE SHOULD I GO?

BAM
THEY WENT OVER THE EDGE!
GO GET THEM! HURRY!
CRUMBLE
HEY.
Shiver
LOOK AT ME.

CLAP

GET A HOLD OF YOUR-SELF!
WINCE
THEN STOP...
...RUNNING AWAY.
YOU OPENED YOUR EYES WITH YOUR OWN STRENGTH, RIGHT?
THIS BODY...
...ISN'T COMPLETELY EMPTY YET, RIGHT?
......!
clink
DO YOU REMEMBER THIS?

EVEN AFTER THE GRAND SINKER,
YOU ALWAYS WORE IT.
...WANT TO KNOW WHY YOU LEFT THIS BEHIND.
NO MATTER WHAT, I BELIEVE IN THE LIFE THAT YOU CHOSE.
I GAVE...
...THIS TO YOU.
Lift
BUT IF THERE'S SOMETHING THAT'S BEEN HURTING YOU...
I DON'T...
clink

DON'T RUN AWAY ANYMORE.
IF YOU STOP RUNNING AND STAND ON YOUR OWN TWO FEET,
THEN NO MATTER WHERE YOU GO, OR WHAT YOU GO THROUGH...
...I WILL ALWAYS CATCH UP TO YOU.
WHERE WAS I PLANNING TO GO?
GOT IT?
THIS WARMTH.
HOW COULD I...

...EVER ESCAPE IT?
GOOD GIRL!
Oh, but don't fall anymore, okay?
It's bad for my heart.
Nod
Can you stand?
WHAT...

...WAS I RUNNING AWAY FROM?
TING
BAM
BAM
BAM
GO!
GET THEM!
POINT
Sizzle
drip
drip
DAMMIT.

DON'T YOU GUYS KNOW THAT IF YOU INTERFERE WITH TRUE LOVE,
YOU'LL SUFFER FOR IT IN YOUR NEXT LIFE?
......!
YOU HAVEN'T FORGOTTEN EVERYTHING I SAID, RIGHT?
......!?
I DIDN'T HAVE A LOT OF SIDE EFFECTS FROM THE RESEARCH, SO I SNUCK OUT A LOT.
SO I KNOW THE LAYOUT OF THE RESEARCH FACILITY PRETTY WELL.
That's how I knew which way to go.
I'LL TAKE CARE OF THESE GUYS.
CAN YOU...
...GET OUT ON YOUR OWN?

Shake
WHY...
GO INTO THAT BACK CORRIDOR.
FOLLOW THE SIGNS ON THE WALL.
IT LEADS TO THE HALL THAT TAKES YOU OUTSIDE.
A-211
I'M GOING KINDA NUMB HERE.
DON'T WORRY, I'LL CATCH UP.
Wheeze
WHY DON'T YOU...
...TRUST ME A LITTLE?
...DON'T I...

Squeeze
...REMEMBER THIS PERSON?

CLICK
GRIN
BOOM
!!
DON'T WORRY.

I'LL ALWAYS CATCH UP.
clink
GRIP
I SHOULD GO.
...KNOWS EVERY-THING.
IF SHE...

THEN SHE CAN TELL ME.
THESE BROKEN MEMORIES.
WHICH PARTS DO I REALLY NEED?
WHERE I SHOULD BE.
WHAT I SHOULD DO.
I'M NOT AFRAID.
NO MATTER WHO I AM, I'LL STAND ON MY OWN TWO FEET.
!
TAP
huff
huff
THE LIGHT IS STILL HERE.

...THAT POWER?
TELL ME,
CLICK
ATSUMA-KUN.
....

TAP
THUD
—……
WHAT HAPPENED...
twitch
twitch
...TO YOUR POWER?
huff
huff
WHAT WAS...

BAM
THUD
GAH!

THAT LIGHT WILL NEVER CHANGE...
...AND WILL ALWAYS BE HERE.

I THOUGHT I WAS DONE FOR.
HUFF
HUFF
ALL I COULD THINK...
...WAS THAT I CAN'T GIVE UP NOW.
I DON'T KNOW WHAT HAPPENED.
WHAT DID I DO...
RING
...TO THAT GUY?

Chapter
28 distant love

WHEN YOU TOUCHED HIM, LORD HYDE DROPPED.
AT THE SAME TIME, YOUR RIGHT ARM...
...SHATTERED LIKE IT WAS BLOWN APART FROM THE INSIDE.
I DON'T KNOW...
...WHAT THAT WAS.
STOMP
CRACK
CLICK

UGH!
Hahah
HOW SAD.
AT NOA, YOU HAD...
...THE STRENGTH THAT EVERYONE FEARED.
GRIND
BUT ONCE YOU LOST THE TOHSU, YOU BECAME A NORMAL HUMAN BEING.
YOU CAN'T HURT ME ANYMORE.
I HAVE...
...NO REASON TO KILL YOU.

Wheeze
THE ONLY PERSON WHO IS MESSING EVERYTHING UP...
...IS UTSUHO.
Lift
SO...
YOU'RE LETTING ME GO WITH A WARNING?
YOU'RE SO KIND EVEN IN...
...YOUR POSITION.
THUD
NO, NOT KIND.

SHALL I SAY, STUPID?
huff
tap
DON'T GET ME WRONG, ATSUMA-KUN.
I ALREADY TOLD YOU MY PLANS.
huff
tap
GRAB
WHAT WILL YOU DO? JUST STOP HIM?
......!
I DON'T PLAN ON...
...LETTING YOU DO THAT.

Wheeze
WHAT ARE YOU...
...TO UTSUHO?
WHAT DO YOU MEAN?
Whirr
YOU'RE BY UTSUHO'S SIDE.
BUT WHAT FEAR IS MAKING YOU DO THIS?
I DON'T KNOW YOUR CONNECTION WITH UTSUHO.
BUT IF YOU'RE GOING TO FOLLOW HIM...
...JUST STAY IN THE RESEARCH FACILITY.
THERE IS NO NEED FOR YOU TO DO THIS.
HE IS...

UTSUHO HASUMI IS...
...THE ONLY ONE...
...WHO IS JUST LIKE ME.
I WAS BORN AT THE RESEARCH FACILITY.
EVEN WHEN I WAS YOUNG, I ALREADY KNEW...
...THAT I WAS SUPERIOR TO EVERYONE ELSE.
I KNEW THAT I WAS PERFECT FROM THE START.
I WAS BORED IN THE TOWER,
AND IT MADE ME SICK.

NO MATTER HOW DIFFICULT AN ALGORITHM OR RESEARCH PROJECT.
EVEN THE WORDS AND THOUGHTS OF THE ADULTS AROUND ME...
...NEVER EXCEEDED MY EXPECTATIONS.
THERE WAS NOTHING TO INSPIRE ME.
YES.
UNTIL HIM.

THE FIRST TIME I LOOKED DEEP INTO HIS EYES...
...THEY REFLECTED NOTHING BUT DARKNESS.
IT WAS THE FIRST TIME I FELT JOY.
AN EMBODIMENT OF PERFECTION THAT'S ALMOST INHUMAN.
I KNEW THAT HE WAS WORTHY OF EVERYTHING I HAVE.
I BECAME HIS RIGHT-HAND MAN ALL FOR MYSELF.
I WANT TO SEE WHAT HE WANTS TO SEE.
THAT'S WHY I WANT TO MAKE SURE EVERYTHING IS PERFECT.

EVEN IF IT'S NOT HIS WISH.
YOU'RE LYING.
WOBBLE
Wheeze
YOU'RE NOT HELPING HIM.
YOU SAY YOU GAVE EVERYTHING, BUT YOU CAN'T SIT STILL.
THAT'S BECAUSE...
...YOU DON'T TRUST UTSUHO COMPLETELY.
NO ONE CAN GO UP AGAINST...
...HIS POWER ANYMORE.
NOT EVEN KOJOMARU OR ANY OF THE OTHER KAMUI.
TO UTSUHO,
I'M NOT A THREAT WITHOUT TOHSU.

SO WHY DID YOU COME HERE?
ARE YOU SCARED OF UTSUHO?
OR OF YOURSELF?
......!
GRIP
WHAM
——!
COUGH
SHE...
...WOULD NEVER MAKE THAT FACE BY UTSUHO'S SIDE.

WHAT ARE YOU...
...AFRAID OF?
IF YOU CAN SEE THE FUTURE,
THERE IS NO NEED TO BE AFRAID.
I ONLY NEED...
CLATTER
SH...

...ONE RIGHT-HAND MAN.
SHUT UP!
BAM
CLICK
huff

THUD
HEY!
LIFT
KOJOMARU!

WHOOSH
LORD HYDE,
STOP NOW!
whoosh

YOU'RE...
......
FLUTTER
THAT WAS...
...A RATHER INTERESTING OPINION,
ATSUMA-KUN.
Heh
YOU CAN'T EVEN GET NEAR HIM.
DO YOU HAVE THE RIGHT TO TALK DOWN TO ME?
......

WE'LL LEAVE.
THE SUN'S SETTING.
AND MY GUN'S BROKEN.
Whirr
STEP
I GUESS...
WHEN YOUR PUNY WISH...
...IS SHATTERED ONCE AND FOR ALL.
...I WILL WATCH FROM MY PLACE.

WHEN YOUR WISH IS SHATTERED ONCE AND FOR ALL.
WHIRR
WHAT...
...HAP-PENED?
WHY...

Huff
WHY DIDN'T YOU KILL HIM?
AND WHAT WAS...
...THAT SYNCHRONIZATION?
YOUR WOUNDS...
SHUT UP!
I'M ASKING YOU...
...A QUESTION...
Thud
KOJOMARU?
ZAP
WHAT?
THAT FEELING.
IT FELT LIKE...

...LIKE...
I DON'T...
TAP
TAP
......
TAP

SLAP
DON'T TOUCH ME...
...WITHOUT PERMISSION.
YOU'RE USELESS IN A PINCH.
THERE'S NO POINT IN KEEPING YOU.
YOU AND ALL THE HUMANS IN THIS CITY...
...ARE JUST PAWNS...
...WHO MUST OBEY US.
Ha!
WHAT ARE YOU AFRAID OF?
AFRAID?
RIDICULOUS.

I'M THE ONLY PERSON WHO'LL SEE HIM ACCOMPLISH IT.
JUST THAT THOUGHT...
...MAKES ME HAPPY.
Float
LIFT
LORD HYDE.

I WILL NOT...
LIFT
...GIVE UP MY POSITION TO ANYONE.
TAP
SO YOU JUST LISTEN TO MY ORDERS.
AND WATCH ME UNTIL YOU CAN NO LONGER MOVE.
TAP
STAY WITH ME UNTIL THE END.
SLAM
VROOM
VROOM

PROTECT ONLY ME.
VROOOOOM
twitch
I SENSE SOMETHING.

THE SAME WAVE...
...AS HIM.

ATSU...
...MA?
YOU...
...STAYED IN THE SHELTER?
YOU'RE FREE NOW.
WHAT HAPPENED TO KOJOMARU?
I DON'T KNOW.
HE SPENT ALL HIS ENERGY TO COME BACK HERE.
I CAN BARELY FEEL HIS CONSCIOUS-NESS.
....

WHY DID YOU MAKE THIS CONTRACT?
YOU WILL...
...NEVER UNDERSTAND.
WHAT I WANT ISN'T HERE.
EVEN IF THERE IS NO MIRACLE. EVEN IF I'M REJECTED.
I DON'T WANT ANYTHING BUT HIM.
SO YOU WANT TO KILL HIM?

I CAN'T LIVE WITHOUT HIM.
YOU DON'T UNDER-STAND HOW...
...MEANING-LESS THAT LIFE WOULD BE, DO YOU?
ESPECIALLY YOU.
TAP
SINCE YOU WERE KIND ENOUGH TO SAVE SOMEONE WHO BETRAYED YOU.
BOTH YOU AND SHIKI KNOW THAT, BUT WON'T KILL ME.
YOU TRY TO MAKE ME LIVE WITHOUT HIM.
THIS IS...
...TO REPLACE THE CHAIN CALLED NOA.
RING

A NEW CONNECTION TO HIM.
THAT CONNECTION TO HIM?
...I'LL DO ANYTHING.
YOU DON'T WANT IT.
PLEASE GIVE IT TO ME!
WHEN...
...NOA CRUMBLED,
I THOUGHT...
...THERE WAS SOMETHING WRONG.

UTSUHO SAID THAT THIS WAS THE RESULT OF LIVING AS I WISH.
MAYBE THAT'S TRUE.
BUT I DIDN'T HAVE ANYTHING I WANTED INSIDE ME.
I WAS LOST AND POWERLESS.
IT SPREAD THROUGH MY HEART.
GRIP
I COULDN'T MOVE AND I WAS LOSING CONSCIOUS-NESS.
WHEN I THOUGHT EVERYTHING WAS GOING TO END HERE...
...I REALIZED,
THAT THERE WAS SOMETHING I STILL HAD LEFT.

BUT I SAW YOU.
A CHILD WHO CAN ONLY CRY AFTER LOSING EVERYTHING.
YOU REMINDED ME OF HOW I WAS.
IF I HADN'T SEEN ANYTHING,
I MIGHT NOT HAVE REACHED OUT.
IN MY BLURRED VISION.
I ONLY THOUGHT OF ONE THING.
IF EVERYTHING WAS DESTROYED AND EVERYTHING WAS GONE...
...IF YOU WERE STILL LEFT...
...IN MY HAND...
...THEN...

...I KNEW...
lift
...THAT I COULD LIVE AGAIN.
YOU'RE SELFISH.

DON'T SAVE ME FOR THAT REASON.
YOU HAVE THE BOND OF BEING BROTHERS.
I HAVE...
...NOTHING LIKE THAT!
SLAP
I'M DIFFERENT FROM YOU.
I'M NOT CONNECTED TO ANYONE.
NO ONE NEEDS ME.
I WOULDN'T KNOW...
...HOW YOU FEEL.
TURN
YOU DON'T HAVE TO UNDERSTAND MY FEELINGS.
BUT I KNOW...
...HOW YOU FEEL.

THE PAIN...
...THAT YOU HOLD INSIDE.
YOU TOLD ME...
...THAT I SUFFER BECAUSE I LIE TO MYSELF.
I KNOW IT ALL.
THE CONTRACT YOU CHOSE TO MAKE WITH KOJOMARU.
WILL THAT...

...MAKE YOUR PAIN GO AWAY?
YOU'RE DIFFERENT FROM ME.
BUT...
...YOUR WORDS ALWAYS STAY WITH ME.
THE REASON WHY I COULDN'T LEAVE YOU ALONE...
...WAS PERHAPS...
...BECAUSE I STILL WANTED...

...TO HEAR YOUR VOICE.

YOU'RE STILL...
...SELFISH.
YOU TOO.
YOU SAVED ME WHEN I DIDN'T WANT IT.
hmf
SUMIRE.

I WON'T...
...MAKE ANOTHER MISTAKE...
...WHEN I CHOOSE MY PATH.
ROAR

GLOP

TAP
THE SHAPE...
TAP
...IS CHANGING?
NO ONE CAN STOP IT NOW.
IT LOOKS LIKE THE KIND-HEARTED KING LET SOME FOOD ESCAPE.
BUT IT DOESN'T SEEM AFFECTED AT ALL.
IT LOOKS LIKE NOA FULFILLED ITS DUTY.
OKIKURUMI IS PLANTED AND FED.
THE ONLY THING IT STILL NEEDS TO BEAR ITS FRUIT...
...IS WATER.

CAN YOU HEAR IT,
SHIKI?
THE VOICE BEGGING FOR WATER?
RING
IT'S SAYING THAT IT WANTS WATER...
RING
...TO FILL THE ENTIRE CITY.
!
WHAT DO YOU MEAN?
Heheh
THERE IS NO NEED TO BE AFRAID.
YOU HEARD MY WISH,
AND CHOSE TO STAY HERE.

OKIKURUMI WILL WAKE UP SOON, AND EVERYTHING WILL BE OVER.
THEN...
...I WILL DISAPPEAR FROM SUMIRE'S HEART.
YOU MADE THE CORRECT CHOICE,
SHIKI.
MY HEART...
...!
...HAS ALWAYS BEEN MISSING A PIECE.
TAP

THERE IS NOTHING THAT CAN FILL THE SPACE.
NOTHING WILL FIT IN THIS BODY OF DARKNESS TO MAKE IT WHOLE.
SO EVERYTHING WILL BE...
...DYED BLACK.
MY WISH IS TO RETURN THE WORLD TO NOTHINGNESS.
IF THE MISSING PIECE IS OUT THERE SOMEWHERE...

...I HOPE THAT IT WILL...
...TURN THE SAME COLOR AS THE REST OF MY BODY.

LET'S DESTROY THE WORLD TOGETHER.

Grazie! Ci vediamo!! KAMUI[6] Shingo Nanami.

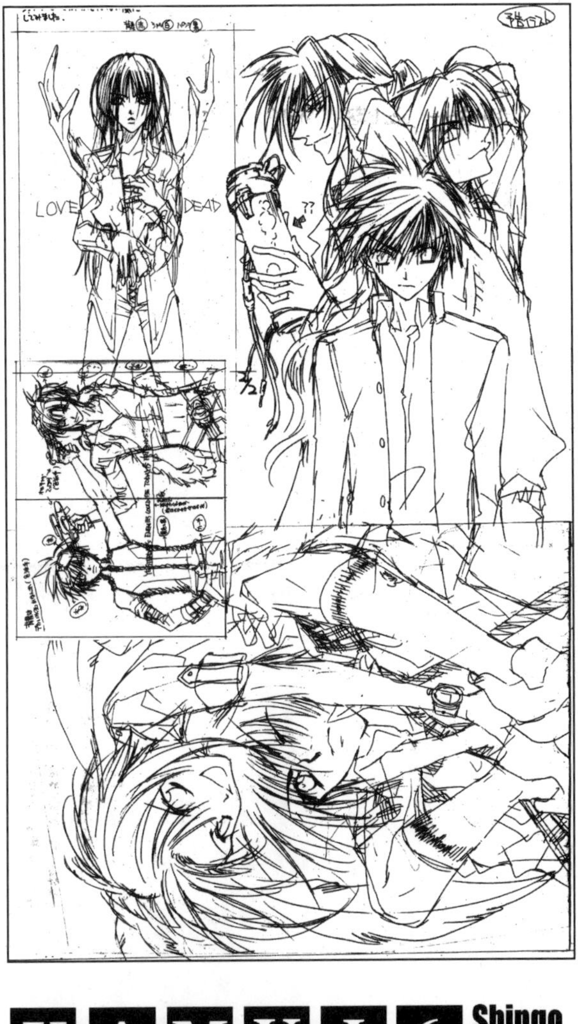

KAMUI 6

Shingo Nanami

PRIVATE SCHOOL NOA ACADEMY, HIGH SCHOOL CAMPUS.
EXPANDING OVER A VAST PLOT OF LAND, WITH ALL THE CUTTING EDGE TECHNOLOGY.
IT'S A PREP SCHOOL IN THE MIDDLE OF THE CITY.
HIGH IN SOCIAL STATUS AND GRAVITAS.
Step
THIS IS...
BUT IN THIS CLOSED SOCIETY,
A NEW WIND IS ABOUT TO STIR THINGS UP A BIT.
...NOA ACADEMY.
Mysterious Transfer Student Atsuma Hasumi (16)
KAMUI School Edition

IN 30-
MINUTES.
Entirely school
grounds.
He needs to get here.
IT'S
TOO BIG,
DAMMIT!
Academy Boat
WHIRR
KAMUI
カムイ
School
Edition

Huff
I...
Huff
I FINALLY MADE IT.
LEAN
No strength left.
Huff
Huff
HEY!
YOU THERE!
TA-DA
BAG INSPECTION!
I HAVE TO CHECK EVERYTHING YOU'RE CARRYING!
Hall Monitor of Justice
Aika Kasuga (16)
WRITE YOUR NAME AND YOUR CLASS HERE...
NO THANKS.
I need to sit down.
CLANG
Beep
Gasp
!!?

WHAT ARE YOU DOING!?
A little scared.
ドキ
BA-DUM
I CANNOT LET INTRUDERS WANDER AROUND!
THAT SWORD IS A VIOLATION OF SCHOOL POLICY. I'M GOING TO CONFISCATE IT!
ドキ
BA-DUM
YEAH, BUT...
...SHOULDN'T YOU BE DOING SOMETHING ABOUT THAT?
CLOP
CLOP
CLOP
WHAT?
THIS
a carriage!?
WHAT IS THIS, CINDERELLA'S CASTLE?
OH, DON'T YOU WORRY YOUNG MAN.
TAP
SHE'S ONLY GOING THROUGH ALL YOUR STUFF.
Swish
THIS IS JUST...

...MY RIDE. ♡
IT'S NOT JUST A RIDE. WHAT IS IT DOING HERE?
YOU CAN'T KEEP DOING THIS, LADY SUMIRE.
...
LAST TIME IT WAS A DOG SLED!
AND THE DOGS GOT LOOSE AND CAUSED A RIOT.
Dog sled!?
BUT I HAVE THE PERMISSION OF THE STUDENT COUNCIL.
RIGHT?
RIGHT, SHIKI?
IS THIS an es-cort ser-vice?
Pop
THAT'S RIGHT.
Queen of the Academy
Sumire Senou (18)

Unfortunate Student Council President Shiki Kenjou (18)
ACCORDING TO TRANSPORTATION CODE 2-11...
HORSES AND CARRIAGES ARE THE SAME CLASS AS BICYCLES.
THAT MEANS...
clop clop clop
...IT DOESN'T LOOK RIGHT BECAUSE YOU'RE SEEING IT LIKE THIS.
IF YOU LOOK AT IT THIS WAY,
キラ
ring ring
Swoosh
IT'S NOT A PROBLEM.
VOILA!
BUT IT'S LIKE THIS.
LET'S GO, SUMIRE.
OKAY. ♪
Not a problem?
The bike looks even less natural.
JUST WAIT A MINUTE...
...YOU CHICK!
I wouldn't want your job.
Shut up.
President needs a write-up.

I GOT UP EARLY TO WAIT FOR YOU.
STEP
AND YOU'RE GONNA GO WITHOUT SAYING HELLO?
DON'T THINK I FORGOT ABOUT THE OTHER DAY.
Delinquent Combo
Reiko the Slasher (age unknown) ↑
AND
← Hyde the Nail-Bat (19)
Oh,
BUT WAKING UP EARLY IS THE CUSTOM...
...OF THE ELDERLY.
GIGGLE
WHO'S ELDERLY!?
You are.
What did you do?
I dunno. ?
YOU DON'T REMEMBER!?
I WON'T LET YOU FORGET IT.
DING DONG DING DONG
Oh, it's time for class.
IT WAS YESTERDAY AT LUNCH.
I MANAGED TO GRAB THE LAST STRAWBERRY FLAVORED MILK.
PREV.
happy
happy
AND AS I WAS ABOUT TO POKE MY STRAW IN...

OH, I AM SO CRAVING SOME STRAWBERRY-FLAVORED MILK TODAY.
Groupie ↓
GLARE
I sense danger.
YES, IT WAS LIKE...
Dead
Poke
Grin
...LOSING YOUR ONLY BELOVED CHILD.
A DEEP SENSE OF EMPTYNESS AND PAIN.
THAT WAS THE LAST STRAW!
Straw-berry flavored milk?
Gone
As expected.
WHERE DID THAT SHE-DEVIL GO!?
Tsk
IT SEEMS...
That self-centered queen of evil left.-
...I'LL HAVE TO SETTLE WITH YOU, TRANSFER STUDENT.

YOU'LL GET A TASTE OF MY DOUBLE-BLADE TOO.
SLASH
CLANG
CLANG
SHINK
I DON'T MIND.
I missed home room anyway.
W-
WELL, YOU HAVE SOME GUTS.
So fast!
LET'S GO THEN.
I don't know these people.
Smoke.

WOoooo
THE GYM IS REMOTE ENOUGH FOR US. YOU CAN'T CALL FOR HELP EITHER.
C'MON!
LET'S GO, TRANSFER STUDENT!
SWICK
TWEET
PATTER
PATTER
PATTER
PATTER
Whistle→
woof
woof
woof
Gasp
A FINGER WHISTLE!?
So what was with the blades!?
THESE DOGS MUST BE...
And why...
DOGS!?

huff
huff
...THAT CHICK'S DOG-SLED DOGS? THE ONES THAT ESCAPED?
Hmph
YOU GUESSED RIGHT.
huff
I TAMED THEM TO PAY BACK THAT WITCH FOR THIS WOUND.
She was bit.
BUT I HADN'T REALIZED HOW HANDY THEY WOULD BE.
Just a hunch.
I BET YOU LIKE ANIMALS.
GULP
Loves them.
Play! Play!
SO, HOW CAN YOU FIGHT WITHOUT INVOLVING THEM?
Urgh
YOU'RE SO EVIL.
RUSTLE
But you can't move either.
Lift
tweet
!!?

WHO'S THAT!?
YIKES!
HEY, REIKO! THE DOGS...
SWICK
ARGH!
WE'LL GET YOU FOR THIS!
woof
woof
I didn't do anything.
I DON'T LIKE PEOPLE WHO GANG UP ON OTHERS.
I DIDN'T NEED YOUR HELP.
whoosh
DON'T GET ME WRONG.
THE DOGS...
...JUST LIKED ME MORE...
...THAN THEY LIKED THOSE TWO.
Carefree Wanderer
Shui Tachibana (18)

WHERE ARE YOU GOING, TRANSFER STUDENT?
I'M GOING TO LOOK AROUND THE SCHOOL THEN GO HOME.
I'm tired now.
THEN BE CAREFUL.
THERE ARE RUMORS OF STUDENT ABDUCTIONS WITHIN THE SCHOOL.
Uh,
Doesn't know what to say.
Okay.
DON'T GO NEAR ANYWHERE TOO SUSPICIOUS.
......
EVEN THOUGH HE WAS TOLD THAT...
...HE GOT LOST.
LOOKS VERY SUSPICIOUS.
Like here.
Cords?
Vines?
RUMORS ABOUT STUDENT ABDUCTIONS...
THAT RED-HEAD.

HE SHOULDN'T WARN PEOPLE WITH STUPID RUMORS.
I'm getting worried for no reason.
slide
BA-DUM BA-DUM
I SHOULD LOOK FOR AN EXIT.
gloop
WHAT THE...
THUMP
WELL, WELL.
GRAB
WHAT A NAUGHTY STUDENT.
!?
LET ME GO!
WHAT WAS THAT THING!?
Mysterious Science Teacher Utsuho Hasumi (26)

THAT DISGUSTING LOOKING OBJECT...
gloop
gloop
HEY! THAT ISN'T WHAT I SAW!
It wasn't a stupid looking rabbit!
Gasp
HEY!
STRIP
YOU HAVE A LOT OF ATTITUDE FOR A TRES-PASSER.
THUD
WHY ARE YOU STRIPPING ME, YOU PERVERT!?
Get away from me!
Well,
IT'S NOT A BAD SIGHT, THOUGH.
MUCH LIKE A FROG IN A MIDDLE OF DISSECTION.
Science teacher
Stare
THAT'S a TERRIBLE analogy!
Don't worry.
IT'S JUST AN EXAMINATION BEFORE THE EXPERIMENT.
THUMP
SO, TRANSFER STUDENT.
Shiver
UGH...

AGGGH!
ROAR
OH.
SORRY, TEACHER.
CRUMBLE
I THINK...
...I ZIGGED WHEN I SHOULDA ZAGGED.
CRUMBLE
!
WHY ARE YOU HERE!?

SEE YA, TEACHER. ♪
BOOM
AGGGGGH!
THAT WAS UNEXPECTED.
drip
FOR YOU...
...TO LOSE YOUR PREY.
FLUMP
Student Council Secretary and Mysterious Spy Yanagi Kuryu (17)
SHALL WE LET HIM GO?
I'll make Shiki pay for the repairs.
I KNOW YOU. I'M SURE YOU HAVE A PLAN.
I HAVE SOME PHOTOS HE MIGHT WANT BACK.
I was following him.
THERE'S NO NEED TO HURRY.
AS LONG AS HE'S AT THIS ACADEMY.
That really is a stupid looking rabbit.
Indeed.

SO,
ちーん。
TA-DA
HOW DID WE END UP HERE AGAIN?
WELL, BECAUSE...
RIDING A MOTORCYCLE ON CAMPUS!?
You can just stay here all night!
DON'T WORRY.
WE'LL GET OUT TOMORROW.
Carefree
She's cute, but tough.
I THOUGHT YOU CAME TO HELP ME.
I TOLD YOU I ZIGGED WHEN I SHOULDA ZAGGED.
Don't get me wrong now.
HE'S USE-LESS!
And I lost my sword.
DON'T BE ALL POUTY.
LOOK ON THE BRIGHT SIDE.

I HOPE YOU MAKE YOURSELF AT HOME SOON,
ATSUMA.
I GUESS.
AND SO...
...A NEW CHAPTER IN HIS LIFE BEGINS.
THE SCHOOL BECOMES A SECOND HOME FOR HIM.

KAMUI School Edition End

KAMUI #6 end

AFTER TALK

Before I realized it, it was already volume 6.

This is thanks to all of you readers and my editors. Thank you very much. Manga does not exist with just the creator. I thank all of you from my heart.

I added rough sketches of color artwork in the extra white pages of this volume. (Some artwork was never used)

If you know which art was used when, you are a KAMUI expert! This volume has more fixes than usual too. I would like to not fix anything from the magazine version... but I'm still not good enough.

I will become better soon!

SCARY THING THAT HAPPENED AT WORK

SEE YOU IN VOLUME 7

I never buy manga that I haven't read already. So when I get letters saying "I never read the book, but saw the cover and bought it!" (a large percentage of KAMUI readers say this) I always think "What a courageous person! There is no way of telling what kind of story it is from the cover! (of course)" I am very thankful when I read those letters.

Please send me letters when you read the manga too!

BROCCOLI BOOKS
1728 S. La Cienega Blvd.
Los Angeles, CA 90035
Attn: Shingo Nanami

SPECIAL THANX to S-chan of art supply store.

カムイ

TRANSLATION NOTES

Pg. 114
Kun - A suffix, usually goes after a boy's name.

Pg. 161
Grazie! Ci vediamo!! - Italian for "Thank you! Till we see each other again!"

Pg. 188
Haku-Hei - Japanese for "empty," as those soldiers are mindless.

AINU CULTURE カムイ

Introduction

Story and elements from KAMUI are deeply rooted in the Ainu culture and religion. Many of the terms including the title are taken directly from Ainu religion. In this and following volumes, we will explore the culture of the Ainu and how it relates to KAMUI, which should provide a broader view and greater appreciation for the story and people behind the book.

The Ainu

The Ainu people are an ethnic group indigenous to Japan's northern island of Hokkaido as well as the Kuril Islands, Sakhalin, and the southernmost third of the Kamchatka peninsula. Today, there are an estimated 150,000 people with some Ainu ancestry living in the world, and of these, most live in Hokkaido.

Although most Ainu live in Japan, they are ethnically different, and have a distinct culture, language, and religious beliefs. In general, their physical build is taller than most Japanese, and Ainu men traditionally keep full beards and mustaches.

The Ainu language is very different from Japanese, although there have been many attempts at linking the two languages. Some proof of this exists in the few words that the two languages share between each other. The Ainu do not have a written language and very few people of Ainu ancestry are fluent in the Ainu language anymore, instead speaking Japanese which is more prevalent. For an example of Ainu language, see chapter 17. The ancient language spoken here by Utsuho is actually Ainu.

The Ainu religion is both pantheistic and animistic. In other words, they believe in many spirits or gods and that these many gods inhabit various natural objects. For instance, the god of the mountains resides in the mountains. Animals were considered to be visitors from other worlds that took on the appearance of animals. Similarly, Shinto, Japan's native religion, is also pantheistic and animistic but differs in other respects. The term "kamui," or "kamuy," is from the Ainu tongue, and more or less means "divine beings." It is interesting to note that the Japanese word for god is "kami," and that the two words are likely related. Kamui have a hierarchy, with some gods having greater importance than others. For example the female god of fire is the most important god in their homes with many offerings being made to her. Kamui are also considered immortal, and are thought to return to their home called "kamui mosir," or "land of the gods."

KAMUI

VOLUME 7 PREVIEW カムイ

7

Sumire and Kojomaru successfully recovered Kojomaru's sword "body," and also managed to free Shui and Aika from Okikurumi. But Shui is captured by Utsuho when he is forced to separate from Aika. Meanwhile Atsuma has repelled the attack of Yanagi and Hyde, displaying a power that no one has seen before, but that leaves his body blackened. What is this power that not even the elders knew existed? And will he be able to use it to rescue Shui and stop Utsuho's plan?

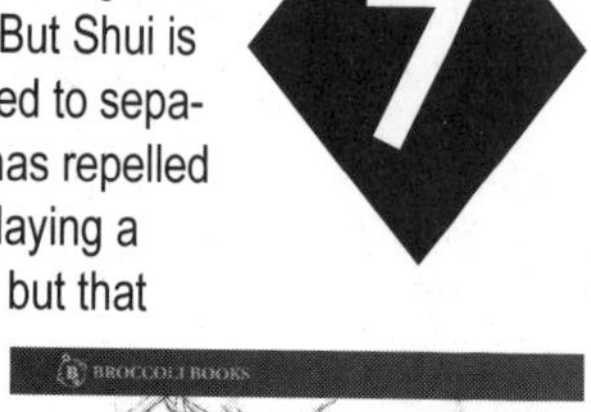

spark
THE AIR SURROUNDING ATSUMA...
ring!
... CHANGED...
I WON'T LET MYSELF FEEL THE SAME PAIN AGAIN!
BOOM!
HE ABSORBED THE TOHSU...

AGH.
AH.
IF YOU'RE CONCERNED ABOUT HIS POWERS,
AH.
YOU SHOULD CHECK IT OUT WITH YOUR OWN EYES.
... OF THE HAKU-HEI SOLDIERS !?
craackle
ARGH.
craackle
NO,
THAT IS...

Bzz...
Bzz...
AGH!
IS HE...
AGH!
AHH!
ABSORBING THE TOHSU!?
AHH!

IS HE...
SWALLOWING THE TOHSU!?
Bzz...
Bzz...
Bzz...
URGH
Bzz...
ARGH!
AHH!
crackle
crackle
Bzz...
Bzz...
AHH!
I CAN FEEL IT...
I CAN FEEL THE KAMUI COMING INSIDE MY BODY.
IS THIS MY...
Roar

BOOM!
IS THIS...
ROAR
...ATSUMA'S POWER!?
Read the rest in KAMUI Volume 7, in Spring 2007!

E'S
VOLUME ONE OUT NOW!
BROCCOLI BOOKS DELUXE
E'S
SATOL 01 YUIGA
Kai Kudou is part of an elite organization of psychics known as Ashurum. One day he is sent on a mission to take custody of other unregistered illegal psychics in the city of Gald. However, he strays from his companions and is taken in by Yuuki Tokugawa, an odd-job-man who is currently working for the guerillas who are in opposition to Ashurum. As Kai spends more time with Yuuki and his mysterious sister Asuka, Kai starts to wonder about the purpose of Ashurum–are they trying to protect the psychics or control them?
$9.99 Ages: 16+
© Satol Yuiga / SQUARE ENIX

E'S IS A VERY HANDY WEAPON.
E'S?
ARE YOU FEELING GUILT LIKE A HUMAN?
SQUEAK
I...
CLICK
...AM HUMAN.

I'M ...
YOU MUTANTS CAN...
CAN I REALLY CALL MYSELF HUMAN?
YOU'RE A PSYCHIC LIKE US. YOU'RE NOT LIKE THEM.
AREN'T I?
MU-TANT!
I CAN KILL SO EASILY WITH THESE POWERS.
I DON'T DESERVE TO BE CALLED HUMAN.

What's E'S?

Characters

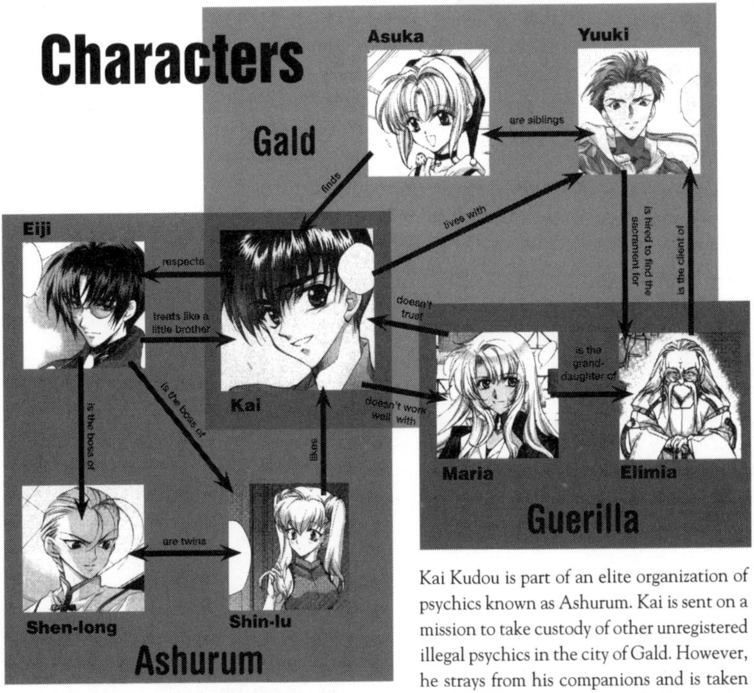

Kai Kudou is part of an elite organization of psychics known as Ashurum. Kai is sent on a mission to take custody of other unregistered illegal psychics in the city of Gald. However, he strays from his companions and is taken in by Yuuki Tokugawa, an odd-job-man who is currently working for the guerillas that are in opposition to Ashurum. As Kai spends more time with Yuuki and his mysterious sisteer Asuka, Kai starts to wonder about the real purpose behind Ashurum.

What secret is Ashurum hiding? What is the truth behind all of their psychics?

Volume 2 coming out in

April 2007!!

BROCCOLI BOOKS *FAN QUIZ!*

How much of a Broccoli Books fan are you? Try taking this test and see what kind of a fan you are! (Answers follow at the end. Try not to peek!)

1. If not the most famous princess alien-hybrid cat-eared girl in the world, then Di Gi Charat's Dejiko is right up there. What phrase does she use to end all of her sentences?

a) D'oh
b) Nyo
c) Nyu
d) Nano da

2. Takuto Meyers, *Galaxy Angel*'s lovable commander, may have a lot of women vying for his attention. How many Angels does he have to juggle in *Galaxy Angel Beta*?

a) 4
b) 5
c) 6
d) 7

3. Kai Kudo is a skilled psychic. But this hero from *E'S* has one weakness. What makes him ill at ease?

a) sweets
b) the dark
c) monsters
d) kryptonite

4. *Disgaea's* resident overlord Laharl has to cement his rule with an iron fist, but he doesn't have to go it alone. Not only does he have demon girl Etna and angel-trainee Flonne by his side, but he also has Etna's army of penguin-like helpers. What are they called again?

a) Weebles
b) Triffids
c) Puchuus
d) Prinnies

5. Okikurumi may be a mythological Ainu hero, but in *KAMUI*, it is depicted as _____.

a) a pot
b) a tree
c) a gem
d) a monkey

6. The pretty boys of *Aquarian Age – Juvenile Orion* may have their following. But they're supposed to be following someone, too. Who is it that they must protect?

a) Yoki Nekogami
b) Mana Kirihara
c) Hikaru Usada
d) Sumire Senou

7. *Yoki Koto Kiku* is a parody-filled black comedy about cute murderous siblings, but it is actually based on what famous Japanese novel?

a) *The Book of Five Rings*
b) *The Inugami Clan*
c) *I Am a Cat*
d) *Before the Dawn*

8. While *KAMUI* is the name of this book, "kamui" is also an Ainu word that means _____.

a) holy
b) human
c) spirit
d) monkey

9. Apricot, or Rico for short, is one of the newest angels in *Galaxy Angel II*. But she's not the first in her family to be on the team. Which of the original Angels is she related to?

a) Milfeulle
b) Mint
c) Ranpha
d) Forte

10. Dejiko has many rivals fighting for the position of number one idol, including Rabi~en~Rose. But who is this little girl who is trying to kidnap her pyo? Leave it to _____!

a) Piyoko
b) Puchiko
c) Yomiko
d) Haruko

Answers: 1. b, 2. c, 3. a, 4. d, 5. b, 6. b, 7. b, 8. c, 9. b, 10. a

1–2 questions right: Broccoli? Isn't that some sort of vegetable?
3–4 questions right: Seconds, please.
5–7 questions right: Can't get enough!
8–10 questions right: Broccoli's my favorite!

AQUARIAN AGE
JUVENILE ORION
オリオンの少年
Realm of Light
Illustration Book
This art book features beautifully drawn, full color artwork from some of Japan's top artists, including Sakurako Gokurakuin, Koge-Donbo, KANAN, PEACH-PIT and Narumi Kakinouchi.
$19.99 Ages: 13+
Special Features
• Full color artwork
• Creator Extra: Nakai Notes featuring extensive information about Aquarian Age – Juvenile Orion
• Translation Notes
Available Now!
© 2006 BROCCOLI Illust. by Sakurako Gokurakuin

Introducing a new manga from Koge-Donbo, the creator of Di Gi Charat and Yoki Koto Kiku.

Coming this June!

こんこん……ここん

Kon Kon Kokon

*working title

Ren just wants to be one of the cool kids, but it doesn't help that secretly he's just a nerdy monster fanatic. That is, until a young girl named Kokon shows up. She claims to be a fox that he had helped years ago and now she wants to return the favor. With the fox girl Kokon by his side, will Ren be able to become the most popular kid in school?

$9.99 Ages: E

DISGAEA 2™
Cursed Memories

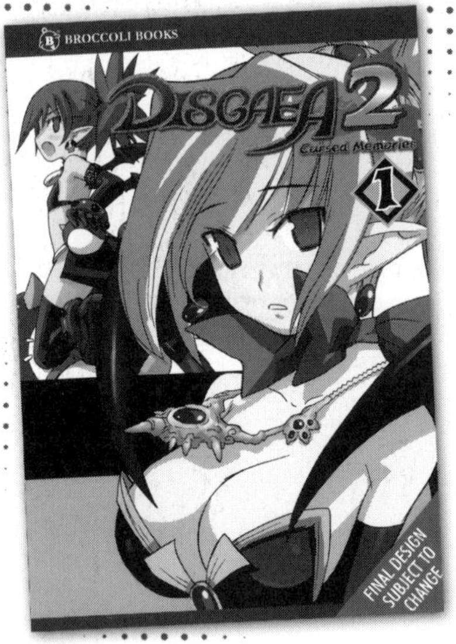

STRANGER IN A STRANGER_LAND

Adell is the lone human being in a world of humans-turned-demons, made by Overlord Zenon. It's Adell's task - and burden - to defeat Zenon and restore his friends and family to their normal selves.

But summoning an Overlord is not easy.

When Adell tries to call Zenon, he ends up with his daughter, Rozalin. Now, bound by contract, Adell promises to take Rozalin back to her father.

However, it will take much more than blind courage to defeat her all-powerful father and save the world.

$9.99 Ages :13+

Voucher inside to receive a Disgaea 2 sticker!

Based on the cult-hit video game Disgaea 2: Cursed Memories!

BRO COMI USA
The Broccoli Books Monthly Webcomic
BROWSE SAMPLE PAGES OF BROCCOLI BOOKS ONLINE!
GO TO BROCCOLIBOOKS.COM AND CLICK ON THE BROCOMI ICON!
UPDATED MONTHLY WITH A DIFFERENT TITLE!
www.broccolibooks.com/webcomic

STOP!

YOU'RE READING THE WRONG WAY!

This is the end of the book! In Japan, manga is generally read from right to left. All reading starts on the upper right corner, and ends on the lower left. American comics are generally read from left to right, starting on the upper left of each page. In order to preserve the true nature of the work, we printed this book in a right to left fashion. Those who are unfamiliar with manga may find this confusing at first, but once you start getting into the story, you will wonder how you ever read manga any other way!

THIS QUESTIONNAIRE IS REDEEMABLE FOR:

KAMUI Volume 6 Dust Jacket

Broccoli Books Questionnaire

Fill out and return to Broccoli Books to receive your corresponding dust jacket!*

PLEASE MAIL THE COMPLETE FORM, ALONG WITH UNUSED UNITED STATES POSTAGE STAMPS WORTH $1.50 ENCLOSED IN THE ENVELOPE TO:**

Broccoli International
Attn: Broccoli Books Dust Jacket Committee
1728 S. La Cienega Blvd
Los Angeles, CA 90035

(Please write legibly)

Name: ______________________________

Address: ______________________________

City, State, Zip: ______________________________

E-mail: ______________________________

Gender: ☐ Male ☐ Female **Age:** _______

(If you are under 13 years old, parental consent is required)

Parent/Guardian signature: ______________________________

Where did you hear about this title?

☐ Magazine
☐ Convention
☐ Internet
☐ Club
☐ At a Store
☐ Other
☐ Word of Mouth

Where was this title purchased? (If known)

____

Why did you buy this title?

____

____

____

____

CUT ALONG HERE

How would you rate the following features of this manga?

	Excellent	Good	Satisfactory	Poor
Translation	☐	☐	☐	☐
Art quality	☐	☐	☐	☐
Cover	☐	☐	☐	☐
Extra/Bonus Material	☐	☐	☐	☐

What would you like to see improved in Broccoli Books manga?

____

Would you like to join the Broccoli Books Mailing List? ☐ Yes ☐ No

Would you recommend this manga to someone else? ☐ Yes ☐ No

What related products would you be interested in? (Check all that apply)

☐ Apparel ☐ Art Books

☐ Posters ☐ Stationery

☐ Figures ☐ Trinkets

☐ Plushies ☐ Other

CUT ALONG HERE

D0205143

Favorite manga style/genre: (Check all that apply)

☐ Shoujo ☐ Anime-based

☐ Shounen ☐ Video game-based

☐ Yaoi

Final comments about this manga:

____

____

____

Thank you!

* While supplies last.
** For residents of Canada, please send an International Reply Coupon (IRC) of $3.00 US made out to "Broccoli International."

All information provided will be used for internal purposes only. We will not sell or otherwise divulge any of the information.

Requests not in compliance with all terms of this form will not be acknowledged or returned. All submissions are subject to verification and become the property of Broccoli International USA. Fraudulent submission, including use of multiple addresses or P.O. boxes to obtain additional Broccoli International USA information or offers may result in prosecution. Broccoli International USA reserves the right to withdraw or modify any terms of this form. Void where prohibited, taxed, or restricted by law. Broccoli International USA will not be liable for lost, misdirected, mutilated, illegible, incomplete, or postage-due mail. Dust jacket offer is only available to residents of the United States and Canada. For updates to the rules and regulations, please see www.broccolibooks.com.